THE CUTE AND CUDDLY GIANT PANDAS

ANIMAL BOOK AGE 5

Children's Animal Books

BABY PROFESSOR

EDUCATION KIDS

Speedy Publishing LLC

40 E. Main St. #1156

Newark, DE 19711

www.speedypublishing.com

Copyright 2017

The giant panda is considered part of the bear family and typically reside in the south central part of China. They are currently considered as a vulnerable to extinct animal, which means they may become extinct if not protected. Read further to learn more about this "cute and cuddly" bear.

WHAT IS A GIANT PANDA?

The giant panda is simply a bear that is white and black. That's correct, it is considered a bear and is categorized in the bear species of Ursidae. It is easily recognizable for its patches of black and white. Its shoulders, legs, ears and eyes are black, with its remaining body being white.

Even though it is fairly large, this giant is not really giant. They can reach up to approximately three feet tall and six feet long while standing on its four legs. The male pandas are typically larger than the females.

The cub does not open its eyes until they are age six to eight weeks and weigh between three to five ounces – about the same size as a candy bar!

WHERE DO THEY LIVE?

They typically live in the Central China mountains. They enjoy the dense moderate forests that have a lot of bamboo. Currently, scientists believe that approximately 2000 pandas live in China's wild. Most pandas that currently reside in captivity are in China. There are approximately 27 giant pandas living in captivity outside of China.

WHAT DO THEY EAT?

Even though they are classified as a carnivore the panda's diet is mostly herbivorous, consisting mostly of bamboo. However, they do have a digestive system of a carnivore and they are not able to digest cellulose correctly and therefore do not obtain much protein or energy from eating bamboo.

On the average, they can eat up to 20 to 30 pounds of bamboo each day. Since their diet is low in nutritional value, they must keep their stomachs full.

Since the region's average temperature has increased they have pushed their habitat to an altitude that is higher and the available space has become limited. Additionally, the timber profit which gains from the harvesting of bamboo, has started to deplete the wild panda's food supply.

Between 1973 and 1984 the wild panda population had decreased in six Asian areas by 50 percent. Although they exist on the herbivore diet, they keep the simple digestive trait of the carnivore. Its round face adapts to the bamboo diet.

Their jaw muscles, which are very powerful, attach from the jaw to the top of their head. Their large molars are able to crush and then grind the bamboo.

There are twenty-five different species of bamboo which are eaten by pandas living in the wild, but it is difficult living in the forest so they also eat dying plants found in a rugged area. There are only a few species of bamboo widespread at the higher altitudes that the pandas now have to inhabit. The leaves of the bamboo have the most protein levels and the stems contain less.

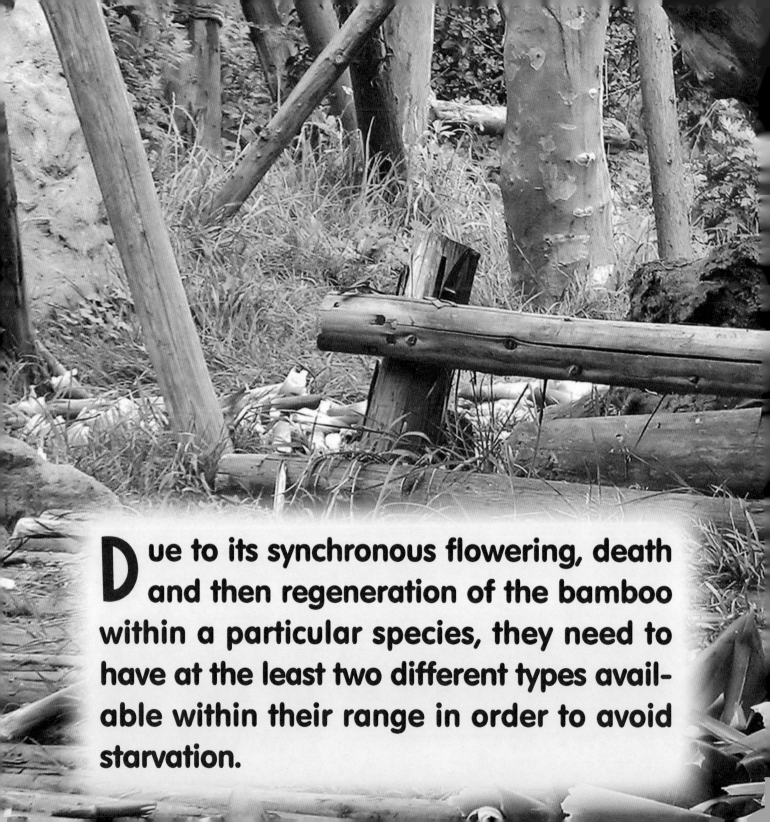

Due to its synchronous flowering, death and then regeneration of the bamboo within a particular species, they need to have at the least two different types available within their range in order to avoid starvation.

Even though they are primarily herbivorous, they still have ursine teeth and can eat eggs, fish and meat, if it is available. When in captivity at zoos, their diet is typically maintained by the zoo, but some might give them special biscuits or dietary supplements.

CONSERVATION

The giant panda is considered an endangered species, and is threatened by its continued loss of habitat and their low birthrate, both in captivity and in the wild.

They have been targeted by local poachers since ancient history and have been poached by foreigners since being introduced in the West.

Beginning in the 1930s, foreigners were not able to poach them in China due to the Second Sino-Japanese War and the Chinese Civil War. However, they continued to be a source for soft furs for the local population.

After 1949, China's population boom put stress on their habitat, which led to the famines and subsequently caused an increase in wildlife hunting, including the pandas. All conservation activities and studies about the pandas were stopped during the Cultural Revolution. After China's economic reform, the demand for the skin of the pandas from Japan and Hong Kong led to their illegal poaching for the black market and these acts were typically ignored at that time by the local officials.

In 1958 the Wolong National Nature Reserve was started by the PRC government in order to prevent the declining number of pandas. However, only a few advances for panda conservation had been made because of inexperience and lack of knowledge in ecology.

Many felt that caging them was the most productive way to save them. As a result, they had been caged if there was any sign of decline and they suffered with horrible conditions. Due to pollution and destruction of their natural habitat, as well as the segregation brought about because of the caging, reproduction became severely limited.

However, during the 1990s, many laws including moving the residents out of the reserves and gun controls, helped with the survival rate for the pandas. With these efforts and better methods of conservation,

they have begun to increase their numbers in a few areas, although they are still considered to be classified as rare species.

Scientists reported in 2006, that the panda population in the wild might have been underestimated at approximately 1,000. Prior surveys used only conventional methods for estimating the number of the population of wild pandas, but now using a newer hi-tech method analyzing DNA from the droppings of pandas, they now believe that this population could be almost 3,000.

While they are still considered en-dangered, it is believed that these conservation efforts are successful. There were 40 panda reserves located in China in 2006, and two decades ago there were only 13 reserves.

THEIR NATURAL ENEMIES

When fully grown, the panda is way too daunting of an adversary for most of their predators, but some can prey on their smaller cubs.

Yellow-threated martens, snow leopards and jackals are some of their potential predators and all of them can be capable of killing and then eating a cub.

In the 2008 movie Kung Fu Panda, Po is a panda that is a kung-fu fanatic and an apprentice noodle-maker and his worst enemy Tai Lung – a kung-fu fighting, fierce snow leopard.

Snow Leopard

Snow leopards, in real life, are also endangered and share similar habitats as the panda and can be a threat to the panda cubs.

CAN THEY FIGHT BACK?

The giant panda is a peaceful and solitary animal and they will typically try to avoid a confrontation, but they do have the means to fight back if they realize an escape is possible.

As cuddly as they appear, they can protect themselves with their physical strength and the power of their jaws and teeth.

They can grow to be 1.5 m in length and weight up to 150 kg.

Even though their large teeth and powerful jaws are for crushing the bamboo leaves and stems, they can also deliver a nasty bite.

They are also very good at climbing, and the cubs are able to get up the trees when they are only six months old.

In addition, they can swim and they do not hibernate for months during winters like bears do.

With these attributes available to them, the giant pandas, once they are grown, can defend against most any predator they come up against.

ARE THEY DANGEROUS?

Even though they appear to be cute and cuddly, and they feed on bamboo for the most part, they can be dangerous around humans.

HOW LONG DO THEY LIVE?

Pandas have been noted to live up to 35 years in a zoo, but typically their life span is closer to 25 to 30 years. It seems as though they cannot live in the wild as long.

WHERE CAN I SEE A GIANT PANDA?

There are currently four zoos in the United States where the giant pandas reside. These zoos include the Memphis Zoo located in Memphis, TN, Zoo Atlanta located in Atlanta, GA, the National Zoo located in Washington, DC and the San Diego Zoo located in San Diego, CA.

Additional zoos which are located throughout the world with Pandas are Ocean Park in Hong Kong, the Chapultepec Zoo in Mexico, Zoologischer Garten Berlin and the Zoo Aquarium in Spain.

There is so much more to learn about the Giant Panda. You might want to ask your parents if you can see the move Kung-Fu Panda, if you haven't already seen it.

If you are lucky enough to live close to one of the zoos that houses them, you can ask them to take you to the zoo. In addition, you can always go to your local library, research the internet, or ask questions of your teachers, family, and friends.

Visit

BABY PROFESSOR
EDUCATION KIDS

www.BabyProfessorBooks.com

to download Free Baby Professor eBooks
and view our catalog of new and exciting
Children's Books

Made in the USA
Columbia, SC
29 November 2017